VANUATU MAP

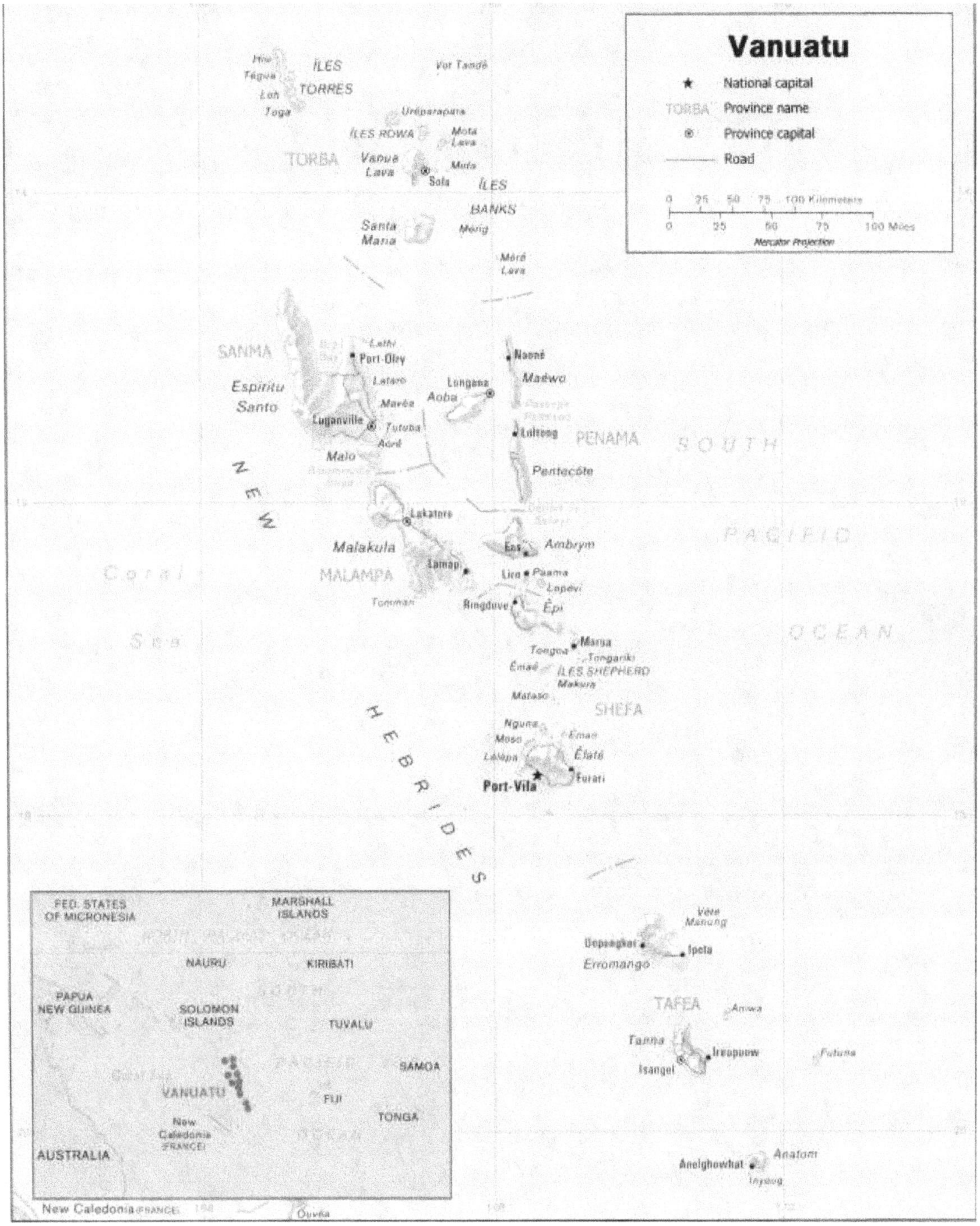

Vanuatu

★ National capital
TORBA Province name
⊛ Province capital
— Road

0 25 50 75 100 Kilometers
0 25 50 75 100 Miles
Mercator Projection

Hiw
Tégua
Loh
Toga
ÎLES
TORRES
Vot Tandé
Uréparapara
ÎLES ROWA
Mota Lava
Mota
TORBA
Vanua Lava
Sola
Muta
ÎLES BANKS
Santa Maria
Mérig
Méré Lava

SANMA
Espíritu Santo
Lathi
Port-Olry
Latoro
Mavéa
Luganville
Tutuba
Aoré
Malo
Lakatoro
Naoné
Longana
Aoba
Maéwo
Lolsong
PENAMA
Pentecôte
SOUTH

NEW
Malakula
MALAMPA
Lamap
Tomman
Lakatoro
Eas
Ambrym
Lien
Paama
Lopévi
Ringdove
Épi
PACIFIC

Coral
Sea
Tongoa
Émaé
Maríya
Tongariki
ÎLES SHEPHERD
Makura
Mataso
SHEFA
OCEAN

HEBRIDES
Nguna
Moso
Lélépa
Émao
Éfaté
Furari
Port-Vila

FED. STATES OF MICRONESIA
MARSHALL ISLANDS
NAURU
KIRIBATI
PAPUA NEW GUINEA
SOLOMON ISLANDS
TUVALU
VANUATU
SAMOA
FIJI
New Caledonia (FRANCE)
TONGA
AUSTRALIA
New Caledonia (FRANCE)
Ouvéa

Uopsagkai
Erromango
Véee Manung
Ipota
TAFEA
Aniwa
Tanna
Isangel
Ircupuow
Futuna

Anelghowhat
Anatom
Inyoug

CONTENTS

PEACE CORPS/VANUATU HISTORY AND PROGRAMS

History and Future of Peace Corps Programming in Vanuatu

Peace Corps Volunteers contribute in very important ways to Vanuatu's national goal of increasing opportunities for Ni-Vanuatu, particularly those living in rural areas. Volunteers support the work of development partners that include government departments, nongovernmental organizations (NGOs), local institutions, and communities. Ni-Vanuatu counterparts work with Volunteers to build capacity and to make projects sustainable beyond the service of the Volunteer. The Peace Corps program in Vanuatu helps:

*   Ni-Vanuatu increase opportunities for education and training and improve the quality of education for young people.

*   Improve the overall health of the Ni-Vanuatu by assisting community-based health care providers in delivering health services to rural communities.

*   Encourage youth and women to take active, leading roles in development.

*   Facilitate the delivery of other important development programs and resources to rural communities and institutions.

Working and living with Ni-Vanuatu at the community level is the theme that transcends the varied assignments of Peace Corps Volunteers. Volunteers are distinguished by their respect for culture, ability to speak Bislama, and willingness to live in some of the most remote areas of the country. They range in age, gender, and experience, but all share a commitment to the goals of the Peace Corps and to the people of Vanuatu.

The work of Peace Corps Volunteers is channeled through two separate projects: the Community Health (CH) project and Vanuatu Information Technology and English Literacy (VITEL) project. These projects share complementary objectives and activities and enable Volunteers to help build the capacity of local institutions and communities while also strengthening links to national development goals and resources.

VITEL Volunteers help improve the quality of education and promote the strengthening of schools by providing formal in-service training to teachers and helping to increase the institutional capacity of schools through the transfer of skills. Volunteers working as primary education teacher trainers and literacy trainers help the Ministry of Education improve the quality of basic education by promoting the enhancement of teaching skills and methodologies, which results in higher literacy levels and effective learning by students in primary schools.

CH Volunteers are currently working closely with health care providers at all levels in the SHEFA, MALAMPA, and PENAMA provinces. Based at the community level, these Volunteers assist local health care providers to implement national and provincial basic health strategies. They focus on reorienting health services to a promotional and preventive model so community members can be directly involved as partners in sharing responsibility for their own health.

History of the Peace Corps in Vanuatu

Despite intermittent talks between the government of the newly independent Republic of Vanuatu and the Peace Corps through the 1980s, a country agreement was not signed until 1989. The first Peace Corps Volunteers arrived in Port Vila in late 1989. During the first four years of its existence (October 1989 to August 1993), the Peace Corps/Vanuatu (PC/V) program was administered by Peace Corps/Solomon Islands.

Following the initial programming assessment trip, it was determined that PC/Vanuatu would concentrate resources and Volunteers in the education sector. The first three Volunteers arrived in 1989 and were assigned to teach either math or science at two different junior secondary schools. They were followed a year later by three additional math and science teachers.

COUNTRY OVERVIEW: VANUATU AT A GLANCE

History

Vanuatu is an independent republic consisting of 83 islands in the southwestern Pacific Ocean. It is located about 3,500 miles southeast of Hawaii and about 1,500 miles northeast of Australia. The capital and largest city is Port Vila, located on the island of Efaté. From the late 19th century until it gained independence in 1980, Vanuatu was governed jointly by France and Great Britain.

Archeological and linguistic evidence supports the commonly held theory that people speaking Austronesian languages first came to the islands about 4,000 years ago. Lapita pottery has been found dating back to 3400 BP, and a graveyard dating back to that time was discovered in the Teouma area on the island of Efate. This was the first of its kind to be discovered in the Pacific.

The first island in the Vanuatu group to be visited by Europeans was Espiritu Santo when, in 1606, Portuguese explorer Pedro Fernandez de Queiros spied what he thought was a southern continent. Europeans did not return until 1768, when Louis Antoine de Bougainville "rediscovered" the islands. In 1774, Captain James Cook named the islands the New Hebrides, a name that lasted until independence.

The majority of Vanuatu's population (78.5 percent) lives in isolated rural areas. The two urban centers have rapidly increased in size, with 15.7 percent of the population residing in Port Vila and 5.8 percent in Luganville. Port Vila, a small but cosmopolitan capital city, contrasts sharply with the rest of the country, with an economy that caters to a significant number of tourists and foreign residents. Much of the tourism economy benefits business owners who come from overseas.

In making the delicate transition from a largely self-sufficient, agriculture-based economy to one that is more market-oriented, Vanuatu is at a pivotal point in its young history. While traditional values and *kastom* (i.e., custom in Bislama) continue to influence society, the pull of the new economy and the lifestyles that come with it have led to a weakened community-based social safety net. The challenge for Ni-Vanuatu is how to strike a healthy balance between the traditional community support system and the rising expectations for jobs, education, health care, and other public services.

Government

In 1906, after years of strife in colonizing Vanuatu, Britain and France developed a unique compromise agreement to jointly administer the islands. Called the British-French Condominium, it provided two completely separate governmental systems, one for English-speaking settlers and one for the French, that came together only in joint court. Melanesians were barred from acquiring citizenship of either power. In effect, this dual system divided Ni-Vanuatu, and aspects of the system remain (e.g., the existence of both English and French educational systems), even though the country now has its own democratic system.

Challenges to the colonial government began in the early 1940s. The arrival of Americans during World War II, with their informal demeanor and relative wealth, was instrumental to the rise of nationalism in Vanuatu. Indigenous beliefs in a mythical, messianic figure named John Frum led to a social movement (popularly referred to as a "cargo cult," related to obtaining industrial goods through magic) that promised Melanesian deliverance.

The first political party, originally called the New Hebrides National Party, was established in the early 1970s. One of its founders was Father Walter Lini, who later became the first prime minister. Renamed the Vanua'aku Pati in 1974, the party pushed for independence, which was realized in 1980.

Economy

Vanuatu's economy is based primarily on subsistence or small-scale agriculture, which provides a living for 65 percent of the population. Agricultural exports (copra, beef, and cocoa), offshore financial services, and tourism are other mainstays of the economy. Tax revenues come mainly from import duties. Mineral deposits are negligible, and the country has no known petroleum deposits. A small light-industry sector caters to the local market.

Economic development is hindered by Vanuatu's poor transportation infrastructure, dependence on relatively few commodity exports, and vulnerability to natural disasters and by the long distances from main markets and between constituent islands. A precipitous decline in world copra prices has reduced the real income of much of the population and has put increased pressure on other resources (i.e., timber, fisheries, and traditional agriculture). The most recent major natural disaster, a severe earthquake in January 2003, on Efaté Island damaged roads, bridges, buildings, and homes extensively in the Port Vila area. Almost all damaged structures have since been repaired.

According to 2010 World Health Organization figures, Vanuatu's population has a median life expectancy of 67 years for males and 70 years for females and a child mortality rate of 36 per 1,000 live births. Forty-eight percent of females and 57 percent of males ages 15 and older can read and write.

The United Nations' Human Development Index, which measures average achievement in terms of longevity, knowledge, and standard of living, ranked Vanuatu 125 out of 187 participating countries in 2011.

People and Culture

The people of the archipelago, who number about 240,000 as estimated from the 2009 census, are known as Ni-Vanuatu. The indigenous population is predominantly Melanesian, with a small number of communities that have a shared Polynesian/Melanesian ancestry. Small numbers of French, British, Australians, New Zealanders, Vietnamese, and Chinese also reside on the islands.

The islands are rugged and isolated, and have some forested peaks several thousand feet high. Vanuatu's land area, scattered over 65 inhabited islands, is about the size of Connecticut, but it is dispersed across an expanse of the equatorial Pacific equivalent to California. The consequent pattern of small settlements with limited outside contact fostered the development of well over 100 distinct Melanesian languages. The most common language, a pidgin known as Bislama, is the language of national unity. English and French are also official languages and are taught in schools throughout the country. Vernacular is the most commonly used language in many communities throughout the archipelago.

Most people are Christians, with the predominant denominations being Anglican, Presbyterian, Seventh-Day Adventist, and Roman Catholic. Many professed Christians also practice some indigenous religious *kastom* and some Ni-Vanuatu adhere solely to the traditional animist beliefs.

Environment

Vanuatu is an island archipelago consisting of approximately 82 relatively small, geologically newer islands of volcanic origin (65 of them inhabited), with about 800 miles north to south distance between the outermost islands. The climate is subtropical, with approximately nine months of warm to hot rainy weather and the possibility of cyclones and three to four months of cool dry weather characterized by winds from the southeast. The land base is very limited (roughly 4,700 square kilometers); most of the islands are steep, with unstable soils, and little permanent freshwater. The shoreline is usually rocky with fringing reefs and no continental shelf, dropping rapidly into the ocean depths.

Vanuatu's relatively fast growing population (estimated at 3.6 percent annually) is placing increased pressure on local resources for agriculture, fishing, grazing, and hunting. Approximately 90 percent of Ni-Vanuatu households fish and consume fish, which has caused intense fishing pressure near villages and the depletion of near-shore fish species. While well vegetated, most islands also show signs of deforestation. They have been logged (particularly of higher-value timber), subjected to wide-scale slash-and-burn agriculture, converted to coconut plantations and cattle ranches, and show evidence of increased soil erosion and landslides.

Fresh water is becoming increasingly scarce and many upland watersheds are being deforested and degraded. Proper waste disposal and water and air pollution are also increasingly troublesome issues around urban areas and large villages. Additionally, the lack of employment opportunities in industry and urban areas and inaccessibility to markets have combined to lock rural families into a subsistence or self-reliance mode, putting tremendous pressure on local ecosystems.

RESOURCES FOR FURTHER INFORMATION

Following is a list of websites for additional information about the Peace Corps and Vanuatu and to connect you to returned Volunteers and other invitees. Please keep in mind that although we try to make sure all these links are active and current, we cannot guarantee it. If you do not have access to the Internet, visit your local library. Libraries offer free Internet usage and often let you print information to take home.

A note of caution: As you surf the Internet, be aware that you may find bulletin boards and chat rooms in which people are free to express opinions about the Peace Corps based on their own experience, including comments by those who were unhappy with their choice to serve in the Peace Corps. These opinions are not those of the Peace Corps or the U.S. government, and we hope you will keep in mind that no two people experience their service in the same way.

General Information About Vanuatu

www.countrywatch.com/

On this site, you can learn anything from what time it is in Port Vila how to convert from the dollar to the local currency. Just click on Vanuatu and go from there.

www.lonelyplanet.com/destinations

Visit this site for general travel advice about almost any country in the world.

www.state.gov

The State Department's website issues background notes periodically about countries around the world. Find Vanuatu and learn more about its social and political history. You can also go to the site's international travel section to check on conditions that may affect your safety.

www.politicsresources.net

This site includes links to all the official sites for governments worldwide.

www.geography.about.com/library/maps/blindex.htm

This online world atlas includes maps and geographical information, and each country page contains links to other sites, such as the Library of Congress, that contain comprehensive historical, social, and political background.

www.cyberschoolbus.un.org/infonation/info.asp

This United Nations site allows you to search for statistical information for member states of the U.N.

www.worldinformation.com

This site provides an additional source of current and historical information about countries around the world.

Connect With Returned Volunteers and Other Invitees

www.rpcv.org

This is the site of the National Peace Corps Association, made up of returned Volunteers. On this site you can find links to all the Web pages of the "Friends of" groups for most countries of service, comprised of former Volunteers who served in those countries. There are also regional groups that frequently get together for social events and local volunteer activities.

www.PeaceCorpsWorldwide.org

This site is hosted by a group of returned Volunteer writers. It is a monthly online publication of essays and Volunteer accounts of their Peace Corps service.

Online Articles/Current News Sites About Vanuatu

http://www.topix.net/world/vanuatu

http://www.vanuatu.net.vu

http://www.dailypost.cm.vu

http://www.vanuatunews.com

Recommended Books

1. Bolton, Lissant. *Unfolding the Moon: Enacting Women's Kastom in Vanuatu*. Honolulu, Hawaii: University of Hawaii Press, 2003.

2. Bonnemaison, Joel. *The Tree and the Canoe*. Honolulu, Hawaii: University of Hawaii Press, 1994.

3. MacClancy, Jeremy. *To Kill a Bird with Two Stones: A Short History of Vanuatu*. Suva, Fiji: Institute of Pacific Studies, 2002.

4. Montgomery, Charles. *The Shark God: Encounters with Ghosts and Ancestors in the South Pacific*. Chicago: University of Chicago Press, 2007.

5. Van Trease, Howard. *The Politics of Land in Vanuatu*. Suva, Fiji: Institute of Pacific Studies, 1987.

Books About the History of the Peace Corps

1. Hoffman, Elizabeth Cobbs. *All You Need is Love: The Peace Corps and the Spirit of the 1960s*. Cambridge, Mass.: Harvard University Press, 2000.

2. Meisler, Stanley. *When the World Calls: The Inside Story of the Peace Corps and its First 50 Years*. Boston, Mass.: Beacon Press, 2011.

3. Rice, Gerald T. *The Bold Experiment: JFK's Peace Corps*. Notre Dame, Ind.: University of Notre Dame Press, 1985.

4. Stossel, Scott. *Sarge: The Life and Times of Sargent Shriver*. Washington, D.C.: Smithsonian Institution Press, 2004.

Books on the Volunteer Experience

1. Dirlam, Sharon. *Beyond Siberia: Two Years in a Forgotten Place*. Santa Barbara, Calif.: McSeas Books, 2004.

2. Casebolt, Marjorie DeMoss. *Margarita: A Guatemalan Peace Corps Experience*. Gig Harbor, Wash.: Red Apple Publishing, 2000.

3. Erdman, Sarah. *Nine Hills to Nambonkaha: Two Years in the Heart of an African Village*. New York, N.Y.: Picador, 2003.

4. Hessler, Peter. *River Town: Two Years on the Yangtze*. New York, N.Y.: Perennial, 2001.

5. Kennedy, Geraldine ed. *From the Center of the Earth: Stories Out of the Peace Corps*. Santa Monica, Calif.: Clover Park Press, 1991.

6. Thompsen, Moritz. *Living Poor: A Peace Corps Chronicle*. Seattle, Wash.: University of Washington Press, 1997 (reprint).

LIVING CONDITIONS AND VOLUNTEER LIFESTYLE

Communications

We realize the United States has become an "instant communication" society. When a Volunteer comes to Vanuatu, family members of the Volunteer must adjust their expectations about how often they can communicate. A few of our Volunteers based in semirural communities will have some Internet connectivity, but most Volunteers will have no connection.

Mail

Pre-service training is held on the island of Efaté, north of Port Vila, the capital of Vanuatu. During training, family and friends can send mail to you at the Peace Corps office. The address is:

"Your Name"

Peace Corps/Vanuatu

PMB 9097

Port Vila

Republic of Vanuatu

Although you can collect your mail from the office, the Peace Corps staff usually brings it to the training site.

Once you are sworn in as a Volunteer, you may choose to have your mail sent to your site. Most provincial centers in Vanuatu have a small post office; otherwise, mail can be sent to the Peace Corps office and staff will forward it to your site. Airmail sent from Port Vila takes two to four weeks to reach the United States. The length of time for mail sent from the United States varies, but small envelopes and parcels generally arrive in Port Vila in two or three weeks. If one is lucky, sea freight mail will take around three months.

Telephones

Cellphones have hit Vanuatu, and rural coverage is now at over 85 percent. Two dueling companies, TVL and Digicel, have competed to make the most of Vanuatu's communities reachable by mobile phone. However, the quality of the service varies greatly from place to place, and some Volunteers may still be an hour's walk from mobile service. In remote locations, Volunteers also have a Peace Corps-issued satellite phone as backup communication.

Landlines are still available in rural areas, but are now less reliable due to the use of mobile phones. Most government offices and provincial centres have landlines that are available, and there are still a limited number of "card phones" located throughout the islands.

Computer, Internet, and Email Access

There are a few Internet cafes in the Port Vila area. You can also access email and the Internet at the Peace Corps office's resource center, which has four computers for use by trainees and Volunteers, as well as wireless for personal computers. There is no Internet access at the training site and trainees rarely come to Port Vila.

Housing and Site Location

For the first few days of pre-service training (PST), you will stay near the capital of Port Vila. You will then move to a rural village on Efaté, staying with a Ni-Vanuatu family for the reminder of training. Although some homes in the village use solar power or generators for electricity, you are more likely to use a little solar lamp or candles. At the training site and in most rural villages, households have a rainwater tank, well, or piped water for drinking and showers. Most houses are composed of local materials, including wood, bamboo, palm and coconut leaves, and tin sheets.

Living Allowance and Money Management

All Volunteers receive a monthly living allowance that enables them to live modestly by the standards of those they serve, yet not in a manner that would jeopardize their health and safety. The monthly allowance is intended to cover food, household supplies, clothing, transportation, recreation, entertainment, and incidental expenses such as postage, film, reading materials, stationery, and toiletries.

Toward the end of PST, the Peace Corps will open an account for you at the National Bank of Vanuatu, where your living allowance will be deposited every month. This bank has branches on many of the islands, so it is easy for most Volunteers to access their bank account.

Peace Corps/Vanuatu will provide you with various resources and materials for use during training and service. Normally you are provided with items such as a medical kit, mattress, lantern, sheets, life jacket, and mosquito net. These items are yours to use while you are a Volunteer, but must be returned at the end of your service.

After you take the oath of service at the end of PST, you will receive a settling-in allowance of 40,000 vatu per individual (approximately U.S. $400) or 50,000 vatu per couple (approximately U.S. $500) to purchase household items such as pots, pans, and a stove.

Food and Diet

Vanuatu has an abundance of fruits, root crops, and vegetables. Most island families grow food in their gardens, and food shortages are rare. There are a few markets and numerous stores on the main islands of Santo and Efaté that carry canned goods, meats, spices, fresh vegetables, cheese, cereal, milk, rice, pasta, and chocolate. On other islands, there are fewer stores and markets and few refrigerated products, but you usually can obtain the essentials.

While many of Vanuatu's foods, such as taros, yams, and breadfruit, will be familiar, you are likely to rapidly develop a taste for virtually all of them. Papayas, pineapples, bananas, plantains, and sweet potatoes are abundant during much of the year. Coconut milk and cream are used to flavor many dishes, and you will soon appreciate them as much as the Ni-Vanuatu do. Most food is cooked using hot stones or through boiling and steaming; very little food is fried.

During PST, you will become familiar with Vanuatu's traditional island food (fish, taro, yams, etc.), or *aelan kakae*, by eating it with your host family. You will eventually develop your favorite dishes and learn how to cook some of them, albeit in your own style.

Transportation

In Vanuatu, you will probably do more walking, riding in the back of pickup trucks, flying in small planes, and bouncing around in small boats than you have ever done before. The undeveloped road system, with less than 100 miles of paved roads, consists mainly of dirt tracks suitable only for four-wheel-drive vehicles. Most islands have one or two short airstrips where Air Vanuatu's small planes land at least one a week.

In addition, every island has a small port or wharf where small cargo ships and boats regularly dock. After one arrives at these locations, transportation is usually via pickup truck, foot, or small boat. Port Vila and Luganville have numerous taxis and mass-transit vans that provide good service at a reasonable cost. Peace Corps Volunteers are prohibited from driving or riding on motorcycles.

Geography and Climate

Vanuatu features isolated rural communities scattered among a chain of beautiful, but rugged and lightly populated tropical islands, which extend about 500 miles north and south.

The water temperature ranges from 72 degrees Fahrenheit (22 degrees Celsius) in the winter to 82 F (28 C) in the summer. It is cool between April and September and the days become hotter and more humid beginning in October. The daily temperature ranges from 68 F to 90 F (20-32 C). Southeasterly trade winds occur from May to October. Vanuatu has a long rainy session, with significant rainfall occurring nearly every month. The wettest and hottest months are December through April, which also constitute the cyclone season. The driest months are June through November. Remember, the weather is very unpredictable and the seasons don't always mean anything. It's best to be mentally prepared for warm to hot, humid to wet, weather. Bring a light windbreaker for those cold winter days when the temperature dips down into the low 70s.

Vanuatu has a variety of natural hazards, such as cyclones, volcanic activity, and earthquakes. Cyclones are the only natural event that generally affects the entire country at once in one way or another. Although they can occur at any time of the year, they are most frequent between January and April. You will receive detailed information about how to cope with cyclones and other natural hazards during PST.

Social Activities

During PST you will live with host families. Living with host families is part of Peace Corps' strategy to assist you in fully integrating into the social setting and life of Vanuatu. As a member of the community, surrounded by other people, it will be a challenge to have your own privacy since members of your family will often be around. Your host families will provide opportunities to build other supportive relationships at your site, enabling you to participate in community activities. Social activities usually revolve around a *lafet* (party), which is a time of eating and dancing, perhaps due to a wedding, family gathering, or commonly for church functions or fundraising initiatives. Other social activities can include the drinking of kava at a local bar or *nakamal*. Drinking kava is a common social activity throughout the islands and is enjoyed by both local and expatriate residents. On most islands, kava can be drunk by both men and women; however, there will be other islands or communities that forbid women to drink kava. For the most part, it is a great way of meeting people or having a good *storian* (chat) about current events.

Peace Corps/Vanuatu is headquartered in Port Vila and Volunteers will at one time or another travel to and from there for work-related or personal reasons. Being in Port Vila provides many Volunteers the opportunity to utilize the resource center at the Peace Corps office for Internet access. Port Vila and Luganville are also the two major towns where you will find a variety of restaurants, pubs, and nightclubs for evening entertainment.

Professionalism, Dress, and Behavior

One of the challenges of finding your place as a Peace Corps Volunteer is fitting into the local culture while maintaining your own cultural identity and acting like a professional at the same time. It is not an easy thing to do, and we can only provide you with guidelines.

You are expected to show sensitivity to the culture of Vanuatu in both dress and behavior. A foreigner who wears ragged clothing is likely to be considered an affront. Most Ni-Vanuatu are conservative in their dress, yet casual. Volunteers who are assigned to classrooms, offices, or health posts have a greater need for professional clothing than those who spend most of their time in the field. Professional in Vanuatu does not mean dress suits. Dress is casual, but in more formal or professional settings it may require long trousers and skirts. However, all Volunteers need an assortment of clothing for work and relaxation. You should have at least one or two nice outfits for special occasions, even if your worksite is in a rural area.

Although attitudes about women's dress are more liberal in Port Vila and Luganville, female Volunteers should dress modestly. Wearing loose fitting tops with skirts is a local fashion, so it is worth bringing such blouses with you. If a dress or blouse is transparent, a camisole or slip is necessary. It is never appropriate for women to show bare thighs (except at tourist pools and tourist beaches), and short-shorts for women are considered improper. When swimming in non-resort areas, women should wrap a *lava-lava* (a sarong-like wrap) around their waist. Many female Volunteers find it is most acceptable in rural areas to wear a "Mother Hubbard"—a dress that is sold locally and may be given to you by your PST host family.

Lightweight but durable cotton or cotton-blend clothes are the most comfortable in Vanuatu's hot and humid climate. Local methods of washing clothes can be very hard on them. Note that leather is subject to mold and mildew and elastic tends to lose its elasticity. Since you may not have electricity for an iron, you may have to get used to wearing more wrinkled clothes than you usually do.

In the hot, direct tropical sun, protective hats are a must. You should also bring raingear (a rain hat is especially desirable if you wear glasses) and a windbreaker for cooler weather. You will need some warm clothes, such as sweatshirts and sweaters, for the cooler months, particularly at night.

For most of the year, sandals without socks are the standard footwear for men and women (water-friendly sport sandals not only are very comfortable and durable, but seem to be a Peace Corps tradition). Many Volunteers also like to wear regular shoes and socks in the cooler months. You will be doing a lot of walking, so think comfort and durability when you buy shoes (i.e., light hiking shoes or sneakers). Local people work and play in flip-flops, which are locally available.

All types of clothing are available in Port Vila and Luganville, but it can be expensive. However, many Volunteers find bargains at the secondhand shops in Port Vila and Luganville, which carry good-quality Australian clothes. It is helpful to learn your sizes according to the European metric system.

Personal Safety

More detailed information about the Peace Corps' approach to safety is contained in the "Health Care and Safety" chapter, but it is an important issue and cannot be overemphasized. As stated in the *Volunteer Handbook*, becoming a Peace Corps Volunteer entails certain safety risks. Living and traveling in an unfamiliar environment (oftentimes alone), having a limited understanding of local language and culture, and being perceived as well-off are some of the factors that can put a Volunteer at risk. Many Volunteers experience varying degrees of unwanted attention and harassment. Petty thefts and burglaries are not uncommon, and incidents of physical and sexual assault do occur, although most Vanuatu Volunteers complete their two years of service without incident. The Peace Corps has established procedures and policies designed to help you reduce your risks and enhance your safety and security. These procedures and policies, in addition to safety training, will be provided once you arrive in Vanuatu. Using these tools, you are expected to take responsibility for your safety and well-being.

Each staff member at the Peace Corps is committed to providing Volunteers with the support they need to successfully meet the challenges they will face to have a safe, healthy, and productive service. We encourage Volunteers and families to look at our safety and security information on the Peace Corps website at www.peacecorps.gov/safety.

Information on these pages gives messages on Volunteer health and Volunteer safety. There is a section titled "Safety and Security in Depth." Among topics addressed are the risks of serving as a Volunteer, posts' safety support systems, and emergency planning and communications.

Rewards and Frustrations

Although the potential for job satisfaction in Vanuatu is quite high, like all Volunteers, you may encounter frustrations. Because of financial or other challenges, collaborating agencies do not always provide the support promised. In addition, the pace of work and life is slower than what most Americans are accustomed to, and some people you work with may be hesitant to change practices and traditions that are centuries old. For these reasons, the Peace Corps experience of adapting to a new culture and environment is often described as a series of emotional peaks and valleys.

You will be given a high degree of responsibility and independence in your work—perhaps more than in any other job you have had or will have. You will often find yourself in situations that require an ability to motivate yourself and your co-workers with little guidance from supervisors. You might work for months without seeing any visible impact from, or receiving feedback on, your work. Development is a slow process. Positive progress most often comes after the combined efforts of several Volunteers over the course of many years. You must possess the self-confidence, patience, and vision to continue working toward long-term goals without seeing immediate results.

To overcome these difficulties, you will need patience, maturity, flexibility, open-mindedness, resourcefulness, and a positive attitude. The Peace Corps/Vanuatu staff, your co-workers, and fellow Volunteers will support you during times of challenge, as well as in moments of success. Judging by the experience of former Volunteers, the peaks are well worth the difficult times, and most Volunteers leave Vanuatu feeling they gained much more than they sacrificed during their service. If you are able to make the commitment to integrate into your community and work hard, you will be a successful Volunteer.

Volunteers are usually readily accepted into their community and form lasting friendships. However, it is important to note that traditional customs and beliefs are held dear, especially in rural areas, and change comes slowly. Having to constantly answer personal questions, the lack of privacy, being considered a rich foreigner, and the need to be constantly aware of different social modes can all be frustrating. The Peace Corps is not for everyone.

Creativity, initiative, patience, flexibility, and a high tolerance for ambiguity are necessary attributes in confronting the challenges associated with facilitating change in a new cultural setting. Your dedication can, however, lead to real lasting results that empower community members not only to achieve your project's goals, but also to identify and address other important needs. You are likely to experience the deep satisfaction of having played a role in a grassroots development process that gives the people of Vanuatu greater control of their future.

PEACE CORPS TRAINING

Overview of Pre-Service Training

Pre-service training (PST) is the first event within a competency-based training program that continues throughout your 27 months of service in Vanuatu. PST ensures that Volunteers are equipped with the knowledge, skills, and attitudes to effectively perform their jobs. On average, nine of 10 trainees are sworn in as Volunteers.

PST is conducted in Vanuatu and is directed by the Peace Corps with participation from representatives of Vanuatu organizations, former Volunteers, and/or training contractors. The length of Phase I PST is usually nine weeks, depending on the competencies required for the assignment. Peace Corps/Vanuatu measures achievement of learning and determines if trainees have successfully achieved competencies, including language standards, for swearing in as a Peace Corps Volunteer. After swearing in, Volunteers go to their sites for approximately three months, and then return to Vila for two weeks of sector-specific technical training, called Phase II training.

Throughout service, Volunteers strive to achieve performance competencies. Initially, PST affords the opportunity for trainees to develop and test their own resources. As a trainee, you will play an active role in self-education. You will be asked to decide how best to set and meet objectives and to find alternative solutions. You will be asked to prepare for an experience in which you will often have to take the initiative and accept responsibility for decisions. Your success will be enhanced by your own effort to take responsibility for your learning and through sharing experiences with others.

Peace Corps training is founded on adult learning methods and often includes experiential "hands-on" applications such as conducting a participatory community needs assessment and facilitating groups. Successful training results in competence in various technical, linguistic, cross-cultural, health, and safety and security areas. Integrating into the community is usually one of the core competencies Volunteers strive to achieve both in PST and during the first several months of service. Successful sustainable development work is based on the local trust and confidence Volunteers build by living in, and respectfully integrating into, the Vanuatu community and culture. Trainees are prepared for this through a "homestay" experience, which requires trainees to live with host families during PST. Integration into the community not only facilitates good working relationships, but it fosters language learning and cross-cultural acceptance and trust, which help ensure your health, safety, and security.

Woven into the competencies, the ability to communicate in the host country language is critical to being an effective Peace Corps Volunteer. So basic is this precept that it is spelled out in the Peace Corps Act: No person shall be assigned to duty as a Volunteer under this act in any foreign country or area unless at the time of such assignment he (or she) possesses such reasonable proficiency as his (or her) assignment requires in speaking the language of the country or area to which he (or she) is assigned.

Although Bislama is the national language, there are many other local languages throughout Vanuatu. You will not be taught local languages during PST, but are encouraged to learn the local language of your community during your service.

Technical Training

Technical training will prepare you to work in Vanuatu by building on the skills you already have and helping you develop new skills in a manner appropriate to the needs of the country. The Peace Corps staff, Ni-Vanuatu experts, and current Volunteers will conduct the training program. Training places great emphasis on learning how to transfer the skills you have to the community in which you will serve as a Volunteer.

Technical training will include sessions on the general economic and political environment in Vanuatu and strategies for working within such a framework. You will review your technical sector's goals and will meet with the Ni-Vanuatu agencies and organizations that invited the Peace Corps to assist them. You will be supported and evaluated throughout the training to build the confidence and skills you need to undertake your project activities and be a productive member of your community.

Language Training

As a Peace Corps Volunteer, you will find that language skills are key to personal and professional satisfaction during your service. These skills are critical to your job performance, they help you integrate into your community, and they can ease your personal adaptation to the new surroundings. Therefore, language training is at the heart of the training program. You must successfully meet minimum language requirements to complete training and become a Volunteer. Ni-Vanuatu language instructors teach formal language classes five days a week in small groups of four to five people.

Your language training will incorporate a community-based approach. In addition to classroom time, you will be given assignments to work on outside of the classroom and with your host family. The goal is to get you to a point of basic social communication skills so you can practice and develop language skills further once you are at your site. Prior to being sworn in as a Volunteer, you will work on strategies to continue language studies during your service.

Cross-Cultural Training

As part of your pre-service training, you will live with a Ni-Vanuatu host family. This experience is designed to ease your transition to life at your site. Families go through an orientation conducted by Peace Corps staff to explain the purpose of pre-service training and to assist them in helping you adapt to living in Vanuatu. Many Volunteers form strong and lasting friendships with their host families.

Cross-cultural and community development training will help you improve your communication skills and understand your role as a facilitator of development. You will be exposed to topics such as community mobilization, conflict resolution, gender and development, nonformal and adult education strategies, and political structures.

Health Training

During pre-service training, you will be given basic medical training and information. You will be expected to practice preventive health care and to take responsibility for your own health by adhering to all medical policies. Trainees are required to attend all medical sessions. The topics include preventive health measures and minor and major medical issues that you might encounter while in Vanuatu. Nutrition, mental health, setting up a safe living compound, and how to avoid HIV/AIDS and other sexually transmitted infections (STIs) are also covered.

Safety Training

During the safety training sessions, you will learn how to adopt a lifestyle that reduces your risks at home, at work, and during your travels. You will also learn appropriate, effective strategies for coping with unwanted attention and about your individual responsibility for promoting safety throughout your service.

Additional Trainings During Volunteer Service

In its commitment to institutionalize quality training, the Peace Corps has implemented a training system that provides Volunteers with continual opportunities to examine their commitment to Peace Corps service while increasing their technical and cross-cultural skills. During service, there are usually three training events. The titles and objectives for those trainings are as follows:

- In-service training: *Provides an opportunity for Volunteers to upgrade their technical, language, and project development skills while sharing their experiences and reaffirming their commitment after having served for three to six months.*

- Midterm conference (done in conjunction with technical sector in-service): *Assists Volunteers in reviewing their first year, reassessing their personal and project objectives, and planning for their second year of service.*

- Close-of-service conference: *Prepares Volunteers for the future after Peace Corps service and reviews their respective projects and personal experiences.*

The number, length, and design of these trainings are adapted to country-specific needs and conditions. The key to the training system is that training events are integrated and interrelated, from the pre-departure orientation through the end of your service, and are planned, implemented, and evaluated cooperatively by the training staff, Peace Corps staff, and Volunteers.

YOUR HEALTH CARE AND
SAFETY IN VANUATU

The Peace Corps' highest priority is maintaining the good health and safety of every Volunteer. Peace Corps medical programs emphasize the preventive, rather than the curative, approach to disease. The Peace Corps in Vanuatu maintains a clinic with two full-time medical officers, who take care of Volunteers' primary health care needs. Additional medical services, such as testing and basic treatment, are also available in Vanuatu at local hospitals. If you become seriously ill, you will be transported either to an American-standard medical facility in the region or to the United States.

Health Issues in Vanuatu

On the whole, Vanuatu is a healthy place to live. There are very few poisonous insects or reptiles on land and in the sea. Many of the serious tropical diseases present in other parts of the world are absent or are controlled in Vanuatu. One of the major problems for the local population is malaria. You will be taught how to reduce your risk of catching this disease by using sensible precautions to prevent mosquito bites and by taking prophylactic drugs. Volunteers rarely catch malaria, but those who do can make a full recovery if they seek prompt treatment. You will be given extensive information about malaria during training.

Since weather in Vanuatu is hot and humid much of the time, good personal hygiene is important to prevent skin diseases.

Helping You Stay Healthy

The Peace Corps will provide you with the necessary immunizations, medications, and information to stay healthy. Upon your arrival in Vanuatu, you will receive a medical handbook. During your training, you will receive a medical kit with supplies to take care of mild illnesses and first aid needs. You are expected to take this kit to the training village with you. The contents of the kit are listed later in this chapter.

During pre-service training, you will have access to basic medical supplies through the medical officer. However, you will be responsible for your own supply of prescription drugs and any other specific medical supplies you require, as the Peace Corps will not order these items during training. Please bring a three-month supply of any prescription drugs you use, since they may not be available here and it may take several months for shipments to arrive.

You will have physicals at midservice and at the end of your service. If you develop a serious medical problem during your service, the medical officer in Vanuatu, will consult with the Office of Medical Services in Washington, D.C. If it is determined that your condition cannot be treated in Vanuatu, you may be sent out of the country for further evaluation and care.

Maintaining Your Health

As a Volunteer, you must accept considerable responsibility for your own health. Proper precautions will significantly reduce your risk of serious illness or injury. The adage "An ounce of prevention ..." becomes extremely important in areas where diagnostic and treatment facilities are not up to the standards of the United States. The most important of your responsibilities in Vanuatu is to take the following preventive measures:

Many illnesses that afflict Volunteers worldwide are entirely preventable if proper food and water precautions are taken. These illnesses include food poisoning, parasitic infections, hepatitis A, dysentery, and typhoid fever. Your medical officer will discuss specific standards for water and food preparation in Vanuatu during pre-service training.

Abstinence is the only certain choice for preventing infection with HIV and other sexually transmitted diseases. You are taking risks if you choose to be sexually active. To lessen risk, use a condom every time you have sex. Whether your partner is a host country citizen, a fellow Volunteer, or anyone else, do not assume this person is free of HIV/AIDS or other STDs. You will receive more information from the medical officer about this important issue.

Volunteers are expected to adhere to an effective means of birth control to prevent an unplanned pregnancy. Your medical officer can help you decide on the most appropriate method to suit your individual needs. Contraceptive methods are available without charge from the medical officer.

It is critical to your health that you promptly report to the medical office or other designated facility for scheduled immunizations, and that you let the medical officer know immediately of significant illnesses and injuries.

Women's Health Information

Pregnancy is treated in the same manner as other Volunteer health conditions that require medical attention but also have programmatic ramifications. The Peace Corps is responsible for determining the medical risk and the availability of appropriate medical care if the Volunteer remains in-country. Given the circumstances under which Volunteers live and work in Peace Corps countries, it is rare that the Peace Corps' medical and programmatic standards for continued service during pregnancy can be met.

If feminine hygiene products are not available for you to purchase on the local market, the Peace Corps medical officer in Vanuatu will provide them. If you require a specific product, please bring a three-month supply with you.

Your Peace Corps Medical Kit

The Peace Corps medical officer will provide you with a kit that contains basic items necessary to prevent and treat illnesses that may occur during service. Kit items can be periodically restocked at the medical office.

Medical Kit Contents

Ace bandages

Adhesive tape

American Red Cross First Aid & Safety Handbook

Antacid tablets (Tums)

Antibiotic ointment (Bacitracin/Neomycin/Polymycin B)

Antiseptic antimicrobial skin cleaner (Hibiclens)

Band-Aids

Butterfly closures

Calamine lotion

Cepacol lozenges

Condoms

Dental floss

Diphenhydramine HCL 25 mg (Benadryl)

Insect repellent

Iodine tablets (for water purification)

Lip balm (Chapstick)

Oral rehydration salts

Oral thermometer (Fahrenheit)

Pseudoephedrine HCL 30 mg (Sudafed)

Robitussin-DM lozenges (for cough)

Scissors

Sterile gauze pads

Tetrahydrozaline eyedrops (Visine)

Antifungal cream

Tweezers

Before You Leave: A Medical Checklist

If there has been any change in your health—physical, mental, or dental—since you submitted your examination reports to the Peace Corps, you must immediately notify the Office of Medical Services. Failure to disclose new illnesses, injuries, allergies, or pregnancy can endanger your health and may jeopardize your eligibility to serve.

If your dental exam was done more than a year ago, or if your physical exam is more than two years old, contact the Office of Medical Services to find out whether you need to update your records. If your dentist or Peace Corps dental consultant has recommended that you undergo dental treatment or repair, you must complete that work and make sure your dentist sends requested confirmation reports or X-rays to the Office of Medical Services.

If you wish to avoid having duplicate vaccinations, contact your physician's office to obtain a copy of your immunization record and bring it to your pre-departure orientation. If you have any immunizations prior to Peace Corps service, the Peace Corps cannot reimburse you for the cost. The Peace Corps will provide all the immunizations necessary for your overseas assignment, either at your pre-departure orientation or shortly after you arrive in Vanuatu. You do not need to begin taking malaria medication prior to departure.

Bring a three-month supply of any prescription or over-the-counter medication you use on a regular basis, including birth control pills. Although the Peace Corps cannot reimburse you for this three-month supply, it will order refills during your service. While awaiting shipment—which can take several months—you will be dependent on your own medication supply. The Peace Corps will not pay for herbal or nonprescribed medications, such as St. John's wort, glucosamine, selenium, or antioxidant supplements.

You are encouraged to bring copies of medical prescriptions signed by your physician. This is not a requirement, but they might come in handy if you are questioned in transit about carrying a three-month supply of prescription drugs.

If you wear eyeglasses, bring two pairs with you—a pair and a spare. If a pair breaks, the Peace Corps will replace them, using the information your doctor in the United States provided on the eyeglasses form during your examination. The Peace Corps discourages you from using contact lenses during your service to reduce your risk of developing a serious infection or other eye disease. Most Peace Corps countries do not have appropriate water and sanitation to support eye care with the use of contact lenses. The Peace Corps will not supply or replace contact lenses or associated solutions unless an ophthalmologist has recommended their use for a specific medical condition and the Peace Corps' Office of Medical Services has given approval.

If you are eligible for Medicare, are over 50 years of age, or have a health condition that may restrict your future participation in health care plans, you may wish to consult an insurance specialist about unique coverage needs before your departure. The Peace Corps will provide all necessary health care from the time you leave for your pre-departure orientation until you complete your service. When you finish, you will be entitled to the post-service health care benefits described in the Peace Corps *Volunteer Handbook*. You may wish to consider keeping an existing health plan in effect during your service if you think age or pre-existing conditions might prevent you from re-enrolling in your current plan when you return home.

SAFETY AND SECURITY—OUR PARTNERSHIP

Serving as a Volunteer overseas entails certain safety and security risks. Living and traveling in an unfamiliar environment, a limited understanding of the local language and culture, and the perception of being a wealthy American are some of the factors that can put a Volunteer at risk. Property theft and burglaries are not uncommon. Incidents of physical and sexual assault do occur, although almost all Volunteers complete their two years of service without serious personal safety problems.

Beyond knowing that Peace Corps approaches safety and security as a partnership with you, it might be helpful to see how this partnership works. Peace Corps has policies, procedures, and training in place to promote your safety. We depend on you to follow those policies and to put into practice what you have learned. An example of how this works in practice—in this case to help manage the risk of burglary—is:

- Peace Corps assesses the security environment where you will live and work
- Peace Corps inspects the house where you will live according to established security criteria
- Peace Corp provides you with resources to take measures such as installing new locks
- Peace Corps ensures you are welcomed by host country authorities in your new community
- Peace Corps responds to security concerns that you raise
- You lock your doors and windows
- You adopt a lifestyle appropriate to the community where you live
- You get to know neighbors
- You decide if purchasing personal articles insurance is appropriate for you
- You don't change residences before being authorized by Peace Corps
- You communicate concerns that you have to Peace Corps staff

This *Welcome Book* contains sections on: Living Conditions and Volunteer Lifestyle; Peace Corps Training; and Your Health Care and Safety that all include important safety and security information to help you understand this partnership. The Peace Corps makes every effort to give Volunteers the tools they need to function in the safest way possible, because working to maximize the safety and security of Volunteers is our highest priority. Not only do we provide you with training and tools to prepare for the unexpected, but we teach you to identify, reduce, and manage the risks you may encounter.

Factors that Contribute to Volunteer Risk
There are several factors that can heighten a Volunteer's risk, many of which are within the Volunteer's control. By far the most common crime that Volunteers experience are thefts. Thefts often occur when Volunteers are away from their sites, in crowded locations (such as markets or on public transportation), and when leaving items unattended.

Before you depart for Vanuatu there are several measures you can take to recuce your risk:

- Leave valuable objects in the U.S.
- Leave copies of important documents and account numbers in the U.S. with someone you trust
- Purchase a hidden money pouch or "dummy" wallet as a decoy
- Purchase personal articles insurance

After you arrive in Vanuatu, you will receive more detailed information about common crimes, factors that contribute to Volunteer risk, and local strategies to reduce that risk. For example, Volunteers in Vanuatu learn to:

- Choose safe routes and times for travel, and travel with someone trusted by the community whenever possible

- Make sure one's personal appearance is respectful of local customs

- Avoid high-crime areas

- Know the local language to get help in an emergency

- Make friends with local people who are respected in the community

- Limit alcohol consumption

As you can see from this list, you have to be willing to work hard and adapt your lifestyle to minimize the potential for being a target for crime. As with anywhere in the world, crime does exist in Vanuatu. You can reduce your risk by avoiding situations that place you at risk and by taking precautions. Crime at the village or town level is less frequent than in large cities; people know each other and generally are less likely to steal from their neighbors. Tourist attractions in large towns are favorite worksites for pickpockets.

The following are other security concerns in Vanuatu of which you should be aware:

Creeping or "kriping" is a common event that female Volunteers often experience during their service in Vanuatu. Creeping in Vanuatu is a culturally and socially acceptable form of courtship. It is how someone of the opposite sex will show his interest in you. Sometimes a potential suitor will not directly alert you to their interest in you as they will be embarrassed or afraid of how it may be perceived by either their family or your host family. Therefore, creeping usually entails a night visit outside of your house when everyone, including yourself, may be asleep. The potential suitor may call out your name from outside in a whisper or throw stones or pebbles close to where you are sleeping in order to wake you. Then he may ask you to come outside or allow him inside. Many female Volunteers in Vanuatu are "creeped" and this can be a frightening experience for the unprepared Volunteer. It is important to remember that this is a cultural show of interest that can normally be handled in a culturally appropriate way. During your pre-service training you will receive extensive orientation about "kriping" and how to deal with it when you are a Volunteer.

While whistles and exclamations may be fairly common on the street, this behavior can be reduced if you dress conservatively, abide by local cultural norms, and respond according to the training you will receive.

Staying Safe: Don't Be a Target for Crime

You must be prepared to take on a large degree of responsibility for your own safety. You can make yourself less of a target, ensure that your home is secure, and develop relationships in your community that will make you an unlikely victim of crime. While the factors that contribute to your risk in Vanuatu may be different, in many ways you can do what you would do if you moved to a new city anywhere: Be cautious, check things out, ask questions, learn about your neighborhood, know where the more risky locations are, use common sense, and be aware. You can reduce your vulnerability to crime by integrating into your community, learning the local language, acting responsibly, and abiding by Peace Corps policies and procedures. Serving safely and effectively in Vanuatu will require that you accept some restrictions on your current lifestyle.

Support from Staff

If a trainee or Volunteer is the victim of a safety incident, Peace Corps staff is prepared to provide support. All Peace Corps posts have procedures in place to respond to incidents of crime committed against Volunteers. The first priority for all posts in the aftermath of an incident is to ensure the Volunteer is safe and receiving medical treatment as needed. After assuring the safety of the Volunteer, Peace Corps staff response may include reassessing the Volunteer's worksite and housing arrangements and making any adjustments, as needed. In some cases, the nature of the incident may necessitate a site or housing transfer. Peace Corps staff will also assist Volunteers with preserving their rights to pursue legal sanctions against the perpetrators of the crime. It is very important that Volunteers report incidents as they occur, not only to protect their peer Volunteers, but also to preserve the future right to prosecute. Should Volunteers decide later in the process that they want to proceed with the prosecution of their assailant, this option may no longer exist if the evidence of the event has not been preserved at the time of the incident.

Crime Data for Vanuatu

Crime data and statistics for Vanuatu, which is updated yearly, are available at the following link: http://www.peacecorps.gov/countrydata/vanuatu

Please take the time to review this important information.

Few Peace Corps Volunteers are victims of serious crimes and crimes that do occur overseas are investigated and prosecuted by local authorities through the local courts system. If you are the victim of a crime, you will decide if you wish to pursue prosecution. If you decide to prosecute, Peace Corps will be there to assist you. One of our tasks is to ensure you are fully informed of your options and understand how the local legal process works. Peace Corps will help you ensure your rights are protected to the fullest extent possible under the laws of the country.

If you are the victim of a serious crime, you will learn how to get to a safe location as quickly as possible and contact your Peace Corps office. It's important that you notify Peace Corps as soon as you can so Peace Corps can provide you with the help you need.

Volunteer Safety Support in Vanuatu

The Peace Corps' approach to safety is a five-pronged plan to help you stay safe during your service and includes the following: information sharing, Volunteer training, site selection criteria, a detailed emergency action plan, and protocols for addressing safety and security incidents. Vanuatu's in-country safety program is outlined below.

The Peace Corps/Vanuatu office will keep you informed of any issues that may impact Volunteer safety through **information sharing**. Regular updates will be provided in Volunteer newsletters and in memorandums from the country director. In the event of a critical situation or emergency, you will be contacted through the emergency communication network. An important component of the capacity of Peace Corps to keep you informed is your buy-in to the partnership concept with the Peace Corps staff. It is expected that you will do your part in ensuring that Peace Corps staff members are kept apprised of your movements in-country so they are able to inform you.

Volunteer training will include sessions on specific safety and security issues in Vanuatu. This training will prepare you to adopt a culturally appropriate lifestyle and exercise judgment that promotes safety and reduces risk in your home, at work, and while traveling. Safety training is offered throughout service and is integrated into the language, cross-cultural aspects, health, and other components of training. You will be expected to successfully complete all training competencies in a variety of areas, including safety and security, as a condition of service.

Certain **site selection criteria** are used to determine safe housing for Volunteers before their arrival. The Peace Corps staff works closely with host communities and counterpart agencies to help prepare them for a Volunteer's arrival and to establish expectations of their respective roles in supporting the Volunteer. Each site is inspected before the Volunteer's arrival to ensure placement in appropriate, safe, and secure housing and worksites. Site selection is based, in part, on any relevant site history; access to medical, banking, postal, and other essential services; availability of communications, transportation, and markets; different housing options and living arrangements; and other Volunteer support needs.

You will also learn about Peace Corps/Vanuatu's **detailed emergency action plan,** which is implemented in the event of civil or political unrest or a natural disaster. When you arrive at your site, you will complete and submit a site locator form with your address, contact information, and a map to your house. If there is a security threat, you will gather with other Volunteers in Vanuatu at predetermined locations until the situation is resolved or the Peace Corps decides to evacuate.

Finally, in order for the Peace Corps to be fully responsive to the needs of Volunteers, it is imperative that Volunteers immediately report any security incident to the Peace Corps office. The Peace Corps has established **protocols for addressing safety and security incidents** in a timely and appropriate manner, and it collects and evaluates safety and security data to track trends and develop strategies to minimize risks to future Volunteers.

DIVERSITY AND
CROSS-CULTURAL ISSUES

In fulfilling its mandate to share the face of America with host countries, the Peace Corps is making special efforts to assure that all of America's richness is reflected in the Volunteer corps. More Americans of color are serving in today's Peace Corps than at any time in recent history. Differences in race, ethnic background, age, religion, and sexual orientation are expected and welcomed among our Volunteers. Part of the Peace Corps' mission is to help dispel any notion that Americans are all of one origin or race and to establish that each of us is as thoroughly American as the other despite our many differences.

Our diversity helps us accomplish that goal. In other ways, however, it poses challenges. In Vanuatu, as in other Peace Corps host countries, Volunteers' behavior, lifestyle, background, and beliefs are judged in a cultural context very different from their own. Certain personal perspectives or characteristics commonly accepted in the United States may be quite uncommon, unacceptable, or even repressed in Vanuatu.

Outside of Vanuatu's capital, residents of rural communities have had relatively little direct exposure to other cultures, races, religions, and lifestyles. What people view as typical American behavior or norms may be a misconception, such as the belief that all Americans are rich and have blond hair and blue eyes. The people of Vanuatu are justly known for their generous hospitality to foreigners; however, members of the community in which you will live may display a range of reactions to cultural differences that you present.

To ease the transition and adapt to life in Vanuatu, you may need to make some temporary, yet fundamental compromises in how you present yourself as an American and as an individual. For example, female trainees and Volunteers may not be able to exercise the independence available to them in the United States; political discussions need to be handled with great care; and some of your personal beliefs may best remain undisclosed. You will need to develop techniques and personal strategies for coping with these and other limitations. The Peace Corps staff will lead diversity and sensitivity discussions during pre-service training and will be on call to provide support, but the challenge ultimately will be your own.

Overview of Diversity in Vanuatu

The Peace Corps staff in Vanuatu recognizes the adjustment issues that come with diversity and will endeavor to provide support and guidance. During pre-service training, several sessions will be held to discuss diversity and coping mechanisms. We look forward to having male and female Volunteers from a variety of races, ethnic groups, ages, religions, and sexual orientations, and hope that you will become part of a diverse group of Americans who take pride in supporting one another and demonstrating the richness of American culture.

What Might a Volunteer Face?

Possible Issues for Female Volunteers

Female Volunteers generally face challenges in adapting to and understanding the role of women in Vanuatu, who may appear to be treated as "second-class citizens" or "property." Though Ni-Vanuatu women can hold positions of authority, this does not occur to the same extent as in the United States. Female Volunteers need to understand that their communities may have little experience with women, particularly young women, who have professional roles or live independently of their families and, thus, may expect them to conform to more traditional roles.

Besides receiving more unwanted and inappropriate attention from Ni-Vanuatu men than they get from American men, female Volunteers may also have to work harder than male Volunteers to gain the respect of colleagues in the workplace. The Peace Corps encourages female Volunteers to keep a low social profile and practice discretion in public (e.g., not smoking in public or drinking in bars) to avoid developing an undesirable reputation. You will receive support from the Peace Corps in dealing effectively with these issues.

Possible Issues for Volunteers of Color

Volunteers of color may face special challenges in Vanuatu. While unlikely, you may be the only minority trainee or Volunteer within the Volunteer corps or a particular project. You may not receive necessary personal support from other Volunteers, and there may be no minority members on the Peace Corps/Vanuatu staff to serve as role models.

Once you move to your site, you may work and live with individuals who have no experience or understanding of a non-Caucasian-American culture. In this way, you are provided with a unique opportunity to talk about the diversity of the United States, and the meaning of the word "American." Out of ignorance or because of Vanuatu's current or historical involvement with other countries, you may encounter stereotyped cultural perceptions. You may not be perceived as being American at first because you are not Caucasian. You need to be prepared for staring, pointing, and comments in any community in which you are not known. Finally, while very uncommon, you should be prepared to hear derogatory terms or racial epithets that would be considered completely inappropriate in the United States.

Possible Issues for Senior Volunteers

In Vanuatu there are benefits of being older, as respect comes with age. For the most part you will be accepted by both fellow Volunteers and the Ni-Vanuatu society and younger Volunteers may ask for your advice and support. While some senior Volunteers find this an enjoyable part of their Volunteer experience, others may choose not to fill this role. During training and at their site, senior Volunteers may face challenges due to age, physical adeptness, or health. Staff members will be available to discuss these issues.

On occasion, older Volunteers may not pick up the language as easily as younger Volunteers. Please do not be disheartened by this, but rather with the assistance of the staff, develop a strategy for your individual approach to language learning to reach the required level of proficiency.

Possible Issues for Gay, Lesbian, or Bisexual Volunteers

Vanuatu is conservative by U.S. standards, and homosexual acts are against the law. Because of this, Volunteers who are gay, lesbian, or bisexual have not been able to be open about their sexual orientation. It is advisable to use discretion and common sense before disclosing your sexual orientation to Ni-Vanuatu colleagues and community members.

Homosexuals certainly exist in Vanuatu, but not with the same level of acceptance as there is in the United States. Most homosexuals in Vanuatu have probably migrated to the larger cities, while most Volunteers are posted in smaller communities. Styles of hair, earrings on men, and certain clothing viewed as acceptable in the United States may be considered inappropriate in Vanuatu.

The Peace Corps staff maintains a supportive atmosphere for all Volunteers and will address the concerns of gay, lesbian, and bisexual Volunteers in a sensitive manner.

Possible Religious Issues for Volunteers

Ni-Vanuatu frequently ask Volunteers about their religious affiliation and may invite them to attend a community church. Volunteers not in the practice of attending church may be challenged to explain their reluctance, but it is possible to politely decline if the church or religion is not one of their choices. However, church-going is as much of a social obligation as it is religious, and usually a generous community meal is served afterwards. Ultimately, most Volunteers find effective ways to cope with these issues and come to feel quite at home in Vanuatu.

Possible Issues for Volunteers With Disabilities

As part of the medical clearance process, the Peace Corps Office of Medical Services determined that you were physically and emotionally capable, with or without reasonable accommodations, to perform a full tour of Volunteer service in-country without unreasonable risk of harm to yourself or interruption of service. The Peace Corps/Vanuatu staff will work with disabled Volunteers to make reasonable accommodations for them in training, housing, jobsites, or other areas to enable them to serve safely and effectively.

In Vanuatu, as in other parts of the world, some people may hold prejudicial attitudes toward individuals with disabilities and may discriminate against them. In addition, there is very little infrastructure that can accommodate people with disabilities.

Possible Issues for Married Volunteers

Being a married couple in the Peace Corps has its advantages and challenges. It helps to have someone by your side with whom to share your experience, but there are also cultural expectations that can cause stress in a marriage. The most important thing to remember is that you are in a foreign country with new rules. As long as you remain open-minded you will have a successful service. The possible issues listed below will also depend on the size of the community you will be living in. Sometimes, one spouse may be more enthusiastic about joining the Peace Corps; be better able to adapt to the new physical and/or cultural environment; or be less or more homesick than the other.

Your roles may be different in a new culture. A married man may be encouraged to be the more dominant member in the relationship or to make decisions independent of his spouse's views or to have his wife serve him. He also many be ridiculed if he performs domestic tasks. On the other hand, a married woman may find herself in a less independent role than that to which she is accustomed. She may experience a more limited social life in the community than single Volunteers (since it may be assumed that she will be busy taking care of her husband). She may also be expected to perform "traditional" domestic chores such as cooking or cleaning.

Other possible issues for married Volunteers include the following:

• Competition may cause difficulties; one spouse may learn faster than the other (e.g., language skills, job skills)

• There may be differences in job satisfaction and/or different needs

• Younger Volunteers may look to couples for advice and support

• Married couples are likely to be treated with more respect because the community sees marriage as a responsibility

• You may be asked why you do not have children

- Often there are separate male and female social activities in the villages, and the wife is expected to join in with the women while the husband is with the men

FREQUENTLY ASKED QUESTIONS

This list has been compiled by Volunteers serving in Vanuatu and is based on their experience. Use it as an informal guide in making your own list, bearing in mind that each experience is individual. There is no perfect list! You obviously cannot bring everything on the list, so consider those items that make the most sense to you personally and professionally. You can always have things sent to you later. As you decide what to bring, keep in mind that you have a 100-pound weight limit on baggage. And remember, you can get almost everything you need in Vanuatu.

How much luggage am I allowed to bring to Vanuatu?
Most airlines have baggage size and weight limits and assess charges for transport of baggage that exceeds those limits. The Peace Corps has its own size and weight limits and will not pay the cost of transport for baggage that exceeds these limits. The Peace Corps' allowance is two checked pieces of luggage with combined dimensions of both pieces not to exceed 107 inches (length + width + height) and a carry-on bag with dimensions of no more than 45 inches. Checked baggage should not exceed 100 pounds total with a maximum weight of 50 pounds for any one bag.

Peace Corps Volunteers are not allowed to take pets, weapons, explosives, radio transmitters (shortwave radios are permitted), automobiles, or motorcycles to their overseas assignments. Do not pack flammable materials or liquids such as lighter fluid, cleaning solvents, hair spray, or aerosol containers. This is an important safety precaution.

What is the electric current in Vanuatu?
Vanuatu uses 220-volt current and three-prong "Australian" plugs. Port Vila, Luganville, Lenakel, Isangel, and Norsup are the only areas with central electricity. Inexpensive converter plugs are available in Vanuatu.

How much money should I bring?
Volunteers are expected to live at the same level as the people in their community. You will be given a settling-in allowance and a monthly living allowance, which should cover your expenses. Volunteers often wish to bring additional money for vacation travel to other countries. Credit cards and traveler's checks are preferable to cash. If you choose to bring extra money, bring the amount that will suit your own travel plans and needs.

When can I take vacation and have people visit me?
Each Volunteer accrues two vacation days per month of service (excluding training). Leave may not be taken during training, the first three months of service, or the last three months of service, except in conjunction with an authorized emergency leave. Family and friends are welcome to visit you after pre-service training and the first three months of service as long as their stay does not interfere with your work. Extended stays at your site are not encouraged and may require permission from your country director. The Peace Corps is not able to provide your visitors with visa, medical, or travel assistance.

Will my belongings be covered by insurance?
The Peace Corps does not provide insurance coverage for personal effects; Volunteers are ultimately responsible for the safekeeping of their personal belongings. However, you can purchase personal property insurance before you leave. If you wish, you may contact your own insurance company; additionally, insurance application forms will be provided, and we encourage you to consider them carefully. Volunteers should not ship or take valuable items overseas. Jewelry, watches, radios, cameras, and expensive appliances are subject to loss, theft, and breakage, and in many places, satisfactory maintenance and repair services are not available.

Do I need an international driver's license?

Volunteers in Vanuatu do not need an international driver's license because they are prohibited from operating privately owned motorized vehicles. Most urban travel is by bus or taxi. Rural travel ranges from buses and minibuses to trucks, bicycles, and lots of walking. On very rare occasions, a Volunteer may be asked to drive a sponsor's vehicle, but this can occur only with prior written permission from the country director.

Should this occur, the Volunteer may obtain a local driver's license. A U.S. driver's license will facilitate the process, so bring it with you just in case.

What should I bring as gifts for Ni-Vanuatu friends and my host family?

This is not a requirement. A token of friendship is sufficient. Some gift suggestions include knickknacks for the house; pictures, books, or calendars of American scenes; souvenirs from your area; hard candies that will not melt or spoil; or photos to give away.

Where will my site assignment be when I finish training and how isolated will I be?

Peace Corps trainees are not assigned to individual sites until after they have completed pre-service training. This gives Peace Corps staff the opportunity to assess each trainee's technical and language skills prior to assigning sites, in addition to finalizing site selections with their ministry counterparts. If feasible, you may have the opportunity to provide input on your site preferences, including geographical location, distance from other Volunteers, and living conditions. However, keep in mind that many factors influence the site selection process and that the Peace Corps cannot guarantee placement where you would ideally like to be. Most Volunteers live in small towns or in rural villages and are usually within one hour from another Volunteer. Some sites require a 10- to 12-hour drive from the capital. There is at least one Volunteer based in each of the regional capitals and about five to eight Volunteers in the capital city.

How can my family contact me in an emergency?

The Peace Corps' Office of Special Services provides assistance in handling emergencies affecting trainees and Volunteers or their families. Before leaving the United States, instruct your family to notify the Counseling and Outreach Unit immediately if an emergency arises, such as a serious illness or death of a family member. During normal business hours, the number for the Counseling and Outreach Unit is 800.424.8580; select option 2, then extension 1470. After normal business hours and on weekends and holidays, the Counseling and Outreach Unit duty officer can be reached at the above number. For non-emergency questions, your family can get information from your country desk staff at the Peace Corps by calling 800.424.8580.

Can I call home from Vanuatu?

Local and international calls and texting can be placed from all cellphones, for a price. Trainees have the opportunity to purchase cellphones during the first days of training. Therefore, you should be able to call home during training if you wish.

Will there be email and Internet access? Should I bring my computer?

There is reliable email and Internet access at the Peace Corps office and at Internet cafes in Port Vila and Luganville. Some agencies to which Volunteers are assigned also have Internet access. Some Volunteers bring laptops and access the Internet on their own. Be advised, however, that most Volunteers are assigned to sites that lack regular electric power. If you bring a laptop, you may want to purchase a solar panel with the appropriate adapter to recharge the laptop's battery.

WELCOME LETTERS FROM VANUATU VOLUNTEERS

Hello:

Olsem wanem? My name is Joshua Adeyemi and I am serving in Vanuatu as an IT educator. I want to use this opportunity to tell you a bit about my experience.

I am based in a secondary school on one of the islands that make up Vanuatu. My experience during my first year at site has been varied and unbelievable. I have taught students who had never seen a computer before, taught myself how to repair computers, and assisted in the processing of copra, the main cash source on my island. I have run IT workshops for teachers and chased and killed a trespassing cow with the same teachers. People have woken me up at six in the morning to clean viruses off their ancient laptops; those people have then brought me bags of fresh potatoes in appreciation. I have been in eight-hour staff meetings.

I have felt myself uncertain as a teacher when my students at the end of an hourlong lesson do not understand what I just talked about and been amazed when a kid who was afraid to hold the mouse at the beginning of the year taught himself Microsoft Word. I have climbed up a waterfall with a deputy principal and, later in the day, told him how he could increase the number of computers in the school lab at low cost. I have explained to numerous people that my being American did not mean I could play basketball and then became a source of laughter in my attempts to play handball. My students have failed easy exams and then passed difficult ones. I have had teachers who attempted to misuse the computer lab and overheard those same teachers showing others how to remove viruses from their flash drives. I have been extremely homesick at times and, at other times, I have considered extending my service for one more year.

As I am writing this letter, I reflect back on a particular time at the end of a frustrating day. I went to a nearby village to drink some kava, and I felt like I was in a twilight zone. There I was, sitting down on a bench made out of bamboo, slapping mosquitoes periodically and looking at a kid taking care of the fire used to prepare the copra that will pay his school fees, periodically shooing away dogs attracted to the food we used as kava chasers. I was looking at a black sand beach and hearing the rhythmic sound of waves crashing on said beach and to my left were houses made from weaved bamboo and sitting on my right was a teacher with whom I was discussing the future of IT education in Vanuatu. I looked up and saw a volcano flare off in the distance. It showed up as a red gash in the black sky. Somebody handed me a boiled banana, and at that moment I knew with my entire being that I was in the South Pacific.

If you are an invitee to Vanuatu and you are reading this, I congratulate you. You are coming to an amazing place. Your program and totality of experience might be different; however, if you allow yourself, this could be the best 27 months of your life to date. Vanuatu is a country filled with people. They can be funny, annoying, generous, or unpleasant, but together they make up an amazing country. I will end this letter with something a fellow teacher told me one day when I was stressing out. He looked at me and said *"Jo, yu no kik, everi samting bae I stret nomo."* This means that as you start your service in Vanuatu, if you are worried about something, don't worry about a thing, every little thing is gonna be all right.

Joshua Adeyemi, Peace Corps Volunteer (2009-2011)

Dear Future Peace Corps/Vanuatu Volunteer:

Congratulations! You have been invited to serve in the "happiest place on earth!" Vanuatu is a very unique place–but you will have to wait to get here to see for yourself. One of the questions I get the most often when I meet a new person is, "So, which is better, Vanuatu or America?" I always honestly answer, "They are too different, so I cannot answer your question." (Usually, this conversation is in Bislama, so my answer goes like this: "*O, tufala i difren tumas, mi mi no save ansarem kwestin blong yu.*") I explain that, in America, most people need a job so they can get paid, and consequently pay for food, shelter, and other needs and wants. But in rural Vanuatu, food and shelter is readily available in the bush, all anyone has to do is maintain their gardens and harvest what they need when it is ready. Without the hassle of going to work every day, life is at a different pace here—better known as "*aelan taem.*"

My experiences in Vanuatu have been nothing like I expected; in many ways they have been better. I remember reading my welcome packet when I finally found out where I was going, frantically making lists of things I needed to buy and plans for packing, researching Vanuatu and the South Pacific, and saying my last goodbyes to my friends and family. At night, I would fall asleep, dreaming about my future on an island in the middle of the Pacific Ocean, but none of my dreams were even close to the reality of life here. No matter how well prepared you are, how much research you have done, how many Volunteer blogs you read, you will not fully understand what life is like in Vanuatu until you get here. By all means, do these things, but know that someday you will look back at this time and you will finally understand the meaning of the things you will discover during your preparations.

Even within Vanuatu, life is different in different parts of the country. I remember eagerly waiting for market day (which happened every other week on the island I was originally assigned), where I would meet my fellow island Volunteer and catch up on everything that had happened since we last saw each other. Her community was very different from mine, even though we were on the same island. It was fun catching up, sharing stories about the funny things the *pikinini* (children) said or did, any cultural faux pas we had. We shared aelan-style Western recipes we had made up, talked through the challenges of carrying out our assignments, and celebrated our successes. By the end of our short time together on those market days, I would be breathless and exhilarated after sharing my experiences and hearing about hers.

The best advice I can think to give you is this: Don't worry! Don't worry about what you will pack–after almost four years here, I keep finding things I felt I needed to pack and have not ever used. Vanuatu has some good stores, and you can buy almost everything you need here. Don't worry about learning the language, it will come. I felt as if I did not really learn Bislama until I was in my village, eating with a family, and being asked how it can possibly be daytime in Vanuatu but night in America. Don't worry about what you will be doing when you get here; you will receive enough training to give you a head start, and after you swear in and receive your assignment, your counterparts, host family, community, and/or workplace will help you figure out what is needed and how you can best help.

Something you will probably get tired of hearing during training is "It depends ... " in response to all of your questions about your site. Every place in Vanuatu is just a little bit different and every assignment a Volunteer gets is unique. What sort of work you will be doing, where you live, what you need, all depends on where you are. Some Volunteers are posted in rural and remote areas of the country, while some Volunteers are placed in the capital city. Every situation is different, but as I said before, don't worry! The Peace Corps staff, current Volunteers, your host families and communities, and your fellow trainees will help you figure out the logistics of life when the time comes.

Despite being the happiest place on earth, almost everyone goes through some rough times. There have been some times when I was almost tempted to give up, but I am glad I never did. The Peace Corps really is the "toughest job you'll ever love." I have learned to appreciate even the most frustrating and confusing situations, because even the smallest events can have a large impact on the future. I have learned a lot about myself during my time as a Peace Corps Volunteer, and I have done my best to put my talents (whether I knew they existed or not) to good use.

I hope your experience as a Peace Corps Volunteer in Vanuatu will be one of the most rewarding events in your life, as it has been for me.

Welkam long Vanuatu!

Stephanie Oegema, Peace Corps Volunteer (2007-2011)

Dear Future Peace Corps/Vanuatu Volunteer,

Congratulations! I'm sure it has been a long journey from when you first decided to apply for the Peace Corps to this moment when you're opening your long-awaited Invitation Packet. I remember well the day mine showed up in the mail. And the adventure is only just beginning!

Maybe somewhere in there among all the excitement of knowing the where and when are the questions "What am I getting myself into?" and "Am I ready?"

What you are getting yourself into is an experience unlike any other you have had. Vanuatu is a beautiful place, full of culture and variety. There are beaches and mountains, jungles and urban centers. Every community in Vanuatu is unique in its own way and no two Volunteers have the same experience here. There are beautiful aspects to Vanuatu's culture. And, just as with every culture, there are difficult aspects as well. This experience is going to challenge you, and not in the ways in which you think it will challenge you. But it will absolutely be worth it.

And are you ready for it? Yes and no. No, you can never be 100 percent ready for something like this. But yes, you are as ready as you need to be. You can find everything you need within yourself – the patience to wait out the bad days to get to the good, the strength to find contentment in the little things, and the courage to celebrate the small victories along the way. You will also have an excellent support network here. The Peace Corps/Vanuatu staff, other Volunteers, and fellow trainees will all be there for you and will truly become a new kind of family.

You will have good days and bad days just like anywhere. There will be highs and there will be lows. There will be many times when you love it and there will inevitably be times when you want to leave. My advice to you is this:

Go with the right expectations. It's impossible to be completely free of expectations – our minds naturally seek to fill in the blanks. So do your research. Read up about Vanuatu, go to the Peace Corps/Vanuatu website, read Volunteer blogs, get in touch with RPCVs and ask as many questions as you can think of. Don't be afraid to ask hard or deep questions either. Learn everything you can and then expect that your experience will be different anyway. Expect to be surprised.

Have multiple reasons why you are doing this. On any given day, one of those reasons isn't going to cut it. But if you have two (or several) reasons why you are here, then one or some of the other reasons will allow you to hang in there.

Enjoy what is enjoyable and shake off everything else. A friend in the States just wrote me this advice and it's worth passing on. This is going to be an amazing experience. Relax, be patient, enjoy the great stuff, and shake off everything else!

Welkam long Vanuatu!

Ebs Sutton, Peace Corps Volunteer (2010-2012)

PACKING LIST

This list has been compiled by Volunteers serving in Vanuatu and is based on their experience. Use it as an informal guide in making your own list, bearing in mind that each experience is individual. There is no perfect list! You obviously cannot bring everything on the list, so consider those items that make the most sense to you personally and professionally. You can always have things sent to you later. As you decide what to bring, keep in mind that you have a 100-pound weight limit on baggage. And remember, you can get almost everything you need in Vanuatu.

Many Volunteers put a lot of effort into packing for their Peace Corps service because it is hard to predict what and how much you will need. Keep in mind that most Volunteers bring too much, especially clothing. If you can't live without something, bring it, but remember that you are traveling to a developing country and less is more in many ways. The cultural considerations on the list below are to give you an idea of what you need, but vary for different parts of Vanuatu. It is a diverse country with urban and rural settings. The best thing to do is to prepare for any situation!

Category	Item	(Suggested Quantity) Recommendations or Comments
GENERAL CLOTHING	Belt	(1) Not leather. Even if your clothes fit well, it will be useful if you lose weight!
	Footwear	Everyone in Vanuatu wears sandals or flip-flops. Poor quality ones are found locally. A pair of running/trail shoes may be useful, especially for runners. All weather hiking sandals are good for rainy season and water activities. Bring whatever is most comfortable.
	Hats & Bandanas	Wide brim hats or baseball-type hats are useful for rain/sun. Few are available in Vanuatu. Bandanas are useful and are not easily found in Vanuatu.
	Raingear	A poncho works very well for walking with a backpack. It can rain often in Vanuatu and many people just accept it and get wet. Raincoats are not easily obtainable and most are too hot to wear when it rains. Raincoats are useful when traveling on boats as well. Umbrellas are readily available and inexpensive.
	Swimsuits	(1-2) On the island, Ni-Vanuatu and most Volunteers swim in their clothes. A swimsuit may be useful or more comfortable, especially if you swim often. Women can only wear them in the capital, at resorts, or with a T-shirt and shorts on the island.
	Underwear & Socks	(2 weeks worth) Bring what is comfortable and durable. Some Volunteers give up the practice of wearing underwear; however, those who stick to it appreciate ones from home. Bring socks if you run, are bringing real shoes, or get cold feet. (3-4 pairs, more if you run)

"Western"-style Volunteers may wear "western"-style clothing (jeans, etc.) more often in Port Vila. Short skirts and shorts are still not recommended for women. Remember, most of your time will be spent at your site, so pack appropriately.

	Winter	(1 each) Sweatshirt, long-sleeved shirt, fleece/light jacket, sweatpants/warm pants. These may seem odd things to pack for the South Pacific; however, most Volunteers are glad they brought them come June/July.

They are expensive and difficult to find locally. |
FOR MEN	Pants	(1) Lightweight, casual pants, if necessary for work. Convertible to shorts.
	Shirts	(6-8) T-shirts will be worn most often. For teaching/holding meetings/church, etc. button-down short-sleeved shirts or polos are appropriate. A long-sleeved button-down may be useful.
	Shorts	(5-7) Durable, quick-dry, convertible to pants. (5-7) pairs of boxers–not available locally.
FOR WOMEN	Dresses	(1-2) Casual, loose, long dresses, sleeveless is a plus. Some teachers and professional women wear island dresses, found locally. Roomy but hot!
	Shirts	(4-5) T-shirts or sleeveless (no thin-strap or strapless) shirts will be worn most often with skirts. A button-down shirt or polo may be useful, depending on your profession.
	Shorts	(2-3) Below the knee, quick-dry or board shorts. Ni-Vanuatu women only wear shorts around the house, in the capital, when they go swimming in the sea, or under their island dresses. These are good at night.
	Skirts	(5-7) Loose, calf-length or longer, not see-through, durable. Worn most often with T-shirts. In most places (outside urban areas) women must wear skirts.
	Slips & Bras	(1) Ni-Vanuatu women wear slips (petticoats) under island dresses; cheap ones can be found locally. (5-7) Sport bras or camisole-style bras work well. Bring what is most comfortable in hot weather.

NOTE: It is important to bring a good mix of casual and professional clothing. There are a number of secondhand clothing stores throughout Vila and Santo, where it is possible to find a wide variety of clothing items at affordable prices. Everyone in Vanuatu shops secondhand! And remember that you will handwash all clothes and everything dries poorly when it is wet or humid (most of January through March) so bring enough!

ELECTRONICS

Remember: Vanuatu is a very wet, humid country. The majority of people here still do not have electricity. Volunteers who bring laptops, digital cameras, GPS locators, etc. must find a way to charge them and remove information, as well as store them from the humidity. Electronics are expensive or unavailable in Vanuatu and they are also a potential target for theft.

Batteries

Many Volunteers purchase solar battery chargers and rechargeable batteries. For those who choose not to purchase solar, it is recommended to bring a good amount of batteries. Local batteries do not last long. It is also recommended to try to coordinate your electronics to use the same type of battery. A good mix of solar and batteries is best in case solar chargers break. The amount of sun-energy at sites varies; make certain your solar panel can supply the energy you need (i.e., laptop).

Camera

Digital cameras are very popular, but bring extra batteries and memory cards. Recordable CDs are a good way to store backup pictures. It is best to bring a camera that takes AA or AAA batteries.

Cellphones

Cellphones are available at very affordable prices. Some Volunteers choose to bring phones from the U.S. but you must be sure that they are unlocked.

Flashlights

LED headlamps are the best. Bring extra batteries or rechargeable batteries with a small solar charger. Wind-up torches are also available here. Ni-Vanuatu use kerosene lamps for their homes and waterproof torches for diving at night, etc. Small solar lights are available for sale in Vila.

Music Devices

Music is important to many Volunteers. Some use external amplified speakers, which work very well and will amuse your neighbors. There is a bacterium,which eats away at CDs, so make copies of originals first. A spare music player is handy in case your first one breaks. They are expensive to replace in Vanuatu, and if it is not used, you can usually sell it to another Volunteer.

Plug Adaptors   Vanuatu uses Australia/NZ-style plugs.

Radio

A small battery-operated or hand crank shortwave radio is nice to have. Some Ni-Vanuatu have radios or tape players. Radio reception throughout the country is spotty, but is getting better.

Silica Gel/ Otter Boxes/ Dry Bags

Not readily available in Vanuatu. Dry bags are useful when walking to keep important things protected from rain and humidity.

USB Flash Drive (Memory Stick)

(2-4) Very useful for transporting documents between offices and islands and storing photos. They are available in-country but are expensive.

GENERAL SUPPLIES	Antiseptic Towlettes	Great to have and not available in Port Vila.
	Baggies	Good to keep things dry. Bring many different sizes. Some baggies of varying quality are found in local stores.
	Books	The Peace Corps resource center has books for pleasure and for work. Most Volunteers who bring books do not take them back to the U.S.; they circulate them among Volunteers during service. You may want to bring certain books that you want to read.

There is not a "real book" store in Vanuatu, although there are a couple of stores that sell books. A few places sell very expensive books and dictionaries. Teachers may want a grammar book. There is also a collection of ebooks that Volunteers share with each other. |
	Earplugs	Great for light sleepers or for sleeping through the sound of roosters.
	Eyewear	(1-2) Good-quality sunglasses are very useful here, but may be ruined, so use your discretion. Bring two pairs of prescription eyeglasses (if applicable).
	Gifts	Thank-you gifts for counterparts and training family are appreciated and it's difficult to find good quality, cheap things here. Consider inexpensive watches, playing cards, soccer balls (with needle), etc. But don't stress out too much about this. There are things available in Vila that would be appropriate for gifts as well.
	Kitchen Supplies	It is not necessary to bring pots or pans, dishes, or silverware. You can purchase pots and pans in Vanuatu. Most spices are available but expensive. Bring your favorites, but keep them in their original containers or they will be confiscated by customs. Rubber spatulas, good can openers, and paring knives are recommended, but cheap ones are available. Nalgene bottles with measurements on the side work well for measuring cups. French press/garlic press optional.
	Maps	Good world, U.S., and South Pacific region maps are good ideas, especially for schools or to show people. Make sure your maps are laminated; they are available in Vanuatu but are expensive. An atlas is also a nice reference tool.
	Pictures	It is nice to have pictures of your family, friends, house, street, city, etc. Ni-Vanuatu love to look at pictures and people and things from all over the world.
	Sleeping Gear	Plain bed sheets are available in Vanuatu, as well as thick and thin blankets, although fitted sheets are not. The Peace Corps issues a mattress to each Volunteer at the beginning of training. Mattresses in Vanuatu are approximately 2-inch thick foam pads, twin-sized. Trainees are also given plain sheets and a pillow. A silk cocoon or sleepingbag liner is also nice for traveling in-country because it is lightweight and dries quickly.
	Tools	A Swiss Army knife or Leatherman tool is useful for many Volunteers. They are not available in Vanuatu. Hammers, etc. are available here.

	Travel Alarm	These must run by batteries or solar energy (watches with alarms or alarms on cellphones can suffice).
	Watch	Durable, inexpensive, waterproof/resistant. Insect repellant tends to disintegrate plastic watch bands.
	Backpacks	A sturdy backpack (with rain cover) or duffel bag for three- to four-day trips and a day pack. Most Volunteers use backpacks whenever they travel.
	Office Supplies	Basic supplies are available here: pens, paper, notebooks, etc. The quality may not be what you're used to. Consider a startup supply of pens, a small stapler, a calculator (very expensive here), quality scissors, and duct tape. This also depends on your job assignment. Stickers are great for teachers to bring.
	Water	The water is, for the most part, clean and drinkable; you will not need a water filter here. Drinking bottles are helpful; bottles with measurements on the side are good for cooking.
PERSONAL HYGIENE & TOILETRY ITEMS	Feminine Protection	The Peace Corps provides applicator-less tampons and pads during your service. Otherwise, the selection in Vanuatu is limited and expensive. Bring a start-up supply.
	General	Good tweezers, hair-trimming scissors, nail files, and clippers.
	Prescription Medicines	Bring a six-month supply of all prescription medicines you require.
	Shower Items	Soap, shampoo, conditioner, deodorant, toothbrushes, etc. are available in Port Vila. The selection is not the same as in the U.S. and the price may be higher. Bringing a startup supply is a good idea. If you need something specific, bring it. Biodegradable camp soap is good for you and the environment.
	Toothbrush Holder	Occasionally needs cleaning, but keeps the critters off.
	Towels	(1-2) Quick-dry towels work well, but may still mold. Inexpensive towels are available here.
REC-REATIONAL	Guitar	Cheap ones are available.
	Hammock	Expensive and very limited supply here. Many Volunteers like the nylon variety, and bring them from home.
	Snorkeling Gear	Available, but expensive and of low quality. Mask and snorkel suggested; flippers and reef shoes optional.

Available Upon Arrival	Toilet tissue, toiletry items, sewing kit, hangers, clothesline, etc.
Peace Corps- Issued	Mattress, thin blanket, pillow, sheets, mosquito net, life jacket, insect repellent, medicines, first aid supplies, clothespins, vitamins, bucket, lamp, and more!

PRE-DEPARTURE CHECKLIST

The following list consists of suggestions for you to consider as you prepare to live outside the United States for two years. Not all items will be relevant to everyone, and the list does not include everything you should make arrangements for.

Family
- Notify family that they can call the Peace Corps' Counseling and Outreach Unit at any time if there is a critical illness or death of a family member (24-hour telephone number: 800.424.8580, extension 1470).

- Give the Peace Corps' *On the Home Front* handbook to family and friends.

Passport/Travel
- Forward to the Peace Corps travel office all paperwork for the Peace Corps passport and visas.

- Verify that your luggage meets the size and weight limits for international travel.

- Obtain a personal passport if you plan to travel after your service ends. (Your Peace Corps passport will expire three months after you finish your service, so if you plan to travel longer, you will need a regular passport.)

Medical/Health
- Complete any needed dental and medical work.

- If you wear glasses, bring two pairs.

- Arrange to bring a three-month supply of all medications (including birth control pills) you are currently taking.

Insurance
- Make arrangements to maintain life insurance coverage.

- Arrange to maintain supplemental health coverage while you are away. (Even though the Peace Corps is responsible for your health care during Peace Corps service overseas, it is advisable for people who have pre-existing conditions to arrange for the continuation of their supplemental health coverage. If there is a lapse in coverage, it is often difficult and expensive to be reinstated.)

- Arrange to continue Medicare coverage if applicable.

Personal Papers

- Bring a copy of your certificate of marriage or divorce.

Voting

- Register to vote in the state of your home of record. (Many state universities consider voting and payment of state taxes as evidence of residence in that state.)

- Obtain a voter registration card and take it with you overseas.

- Arrange to have an absentee ballot forwarded to you overseas.

Personal Effects

- Purchase personal property insurance to extend from the time you leave your home for service overseas until the time you complete your service and return to the United States.

Financial Management

- Keep a bank account in your name in the U.S.

- Obtain student loan deferment forms from the lender or loan service.

- Execute a Power of Attorney for the management of your property and business.

- Arrange for deductions from your readjustment allowance to pay alimony, child support, and other debts through the Office of Volunteer Financial Operations at 800.424.8580, extension 1770.

- Place all important papers—mortgages, deeds, stocks, and bonds—in a safe deposit box or with an attorney or other caretaker

CONTACTING PEACE CORPS HEADQUARTERS

This list of numbers will help connect you with the appropriate office at Peace Corps headquarters to answer various questions. You can use the toll-free number and extension or dial directly using the local numbers provided. Be sure to leave the toll-free number and extensions with your family so they can contact you in the event of an emergency.

Peace Corps Headquarters Toll-free Number: 800.424.8580, Press 2, Press 1, then Ext. # (see below)

Peace Corps' Mailing Address: Peace Corps
Paul D. Coverdell Peace Corps Headquarters
1111 20th Street, NW
Washington, DC 20526

For Questions About:	Staff:	Toll-Free Ext:	Direct/Local Number:
Responding to an Invitation:	Office of Placement	x1840	202.692.1840
Country Information:	Sasha Cooper-Morrison x2502 Desk Officer / Micronesia, Palau, Vanuatu scoopermorrison@peacecorps.gov		202.692.2502
	Shelley Swendiman x2523 Desk Officer / Fiji, Samoa, Tonga sswendiman@peacecorps.gov		202.692.2523
Plane Tickets, Passports, Visas, or other travel matters:			
	CWT SATO Travel	x1170	202.692.1170
Legal Clearance:	Office of Placement	x1840	202.692.1840
Medical Clearance and Forms Processing (includes dental):			
	Screening Nurse	x1500	202.692.1500

Medical Reimbursements (handled by a subcontractor):   800.818.8772

Loan Deferments, Taxes, Financial Operations   x1770   202.692.1770

Readjustment Allowance Withdrawals, Power of Attorney, Staging (Pre-Departure Orientation), and Reporting Instructions:

     Office of Staging   x1865   202.692.1865

Note: You will receive comprehensive information (hotel and flight arrangements) three to five weeks prior to departure. This information is not available sooner.

Family Emergencies (to get information to a Volunteer overseas) *24 hours:*

     Office of Special   x1470   202.692.1470

     Services